Date Due

Sept 1990

OCT 2 0 1990	MAY 0 4 1995
NOV 1 0 1990	SEP 1 6 1995
[MAR 0 2 1991]	DEC 0 7 1995
ILL-NH-ND	JAN 3 0 1996
APR 0 9 1991	
MAY 2 0 1992	
OCT 03 1992	
NOV 2 4 1992	
[APR 0 2 1993]	
[MAY 0 8 1993]	
[MAY 2 9 1993]	
NOV 1 2 1993	
FEB 2 4 1994	
Mar 17/94	

BRODART, INC. Cat. No. 23 233 Printed in U.S.A.

Baskets

Baskets

Design Ideas • Techniques and Materials • Step-by-Step Projects

Designs by Richard Kollath
Text by Richard Kollath with Tim Frew
All Photography by William B. Seitz

Weidenfeld & Nicolson
New York

A FRIEDMAN GROUP BOOK

Published in the United States by
Weidenfeld & Nicolson, New York
A Division of Wheatland Corporation
841 Broadway
New York, New York 10003-4793

Library of Congress Cataloging-in-Publication Data

Kollath, Richard.
    Baskets: design ideas, techniques and materials, and
step-by-step projects/Richard Kollath.—1st
ed.
       p.   cm.
    "A Friedman Group book"—T.p. verso.
    Bibliography: p.
    Includes index.
    ISBN 1-55584-305-0
    1. Basket making.   I. Title.
TT879.B3K65 1989   89-30860
746.41'2—dc19   CIP

BASKETS: Design Ideas, Techniques and Materials, Step-by-Step Projects
was prepared and produced by
Michael Friedman Publishing Group
15 West 26th Street
New York, New York 10010

Art Director: Robert W. Kosturko
Designer: Marcena J. Mulford
Photography Editor: Christopher Bain
Production Manager: Karen L. Greenberg

Typeset by BPE Graphics, Inc.
Color separations by Kwong Ming Graphicprint, Ltd.
Printed and bound in Hong Kong by Leefung-Asco Printers, Ltd.

First Edition 1989

10 9 8 7 6 5 4 3 2 1

All photographs © William B. Seitz

DEDICATION

Jason, this book is for you, with love. And to the memory of Marcus Heffelfinger.

ACKNOWLEDGMENTS

This book of baskets has come about through the generous good will and special talents of my friends and associates. I acknowledge their invaluable contribution with gratitude.

To Michael Friedman, Karla Olson, and the collective staff of the Friedman Publishing Group, for their support and general good will.

To Tim Frew, who edited the text of this book with a clarity I applaud and envy.

To Christopher Bain for overseeing the photographic details with precision and kind flexibility.

To Robert Kosturko and his staff for the design of the book and his help with the location photography.

To Bill Seitz for his sensitive and patient care when photographing each basket. As always, working with you was a delight.

To Tim Lee for his able assistance in the photography of this book.

I wish to thank the friends and neighbors who allowed their homes and gardens to be photographed, without which this book would not have it's visual richness.

To Hubert Cutler for his remarkable and poetic garden.

To Joe Eula, an exuberant friend with a splendid home and garden only matched by his vibrant personality.

To Bruce and Jean Morgan for the use of their wonderful home and sensitive collection of objects.

To Stan and Kathy Longyear for their many generous contributions and for growing the best wooden watermelons in town.

To Arthur and Elizabeth Weyhe for sharing the glories of the country house and landscape.

To Richard Kirgan, my neighbor and friend, who so ably works out all the snags when creating with wood. For your time and efforts, I thank you.

To Teri, my wife, who took time off from her own busy schedule to read the rough thoughts and words of this early text, my thanks.

CONTENTS

Introduction ... 8

CHAPTER ONE

Beautiful Baskets ... 14
Basic Tools and Materials ... 16
Developing a Plan ... 20
Basketry Kits ... 22
Coil Baskets ... 22
Vine Baskets ... 26
Log Cabin Baskets ... 30
Bark Cone Baskets ... 34
Wire Planting Baskets ... 36

CHAPTER TWO

Customized Store-Bought Baskets ... 40
Living Baskets ... 42
Antiquing a Basket ... 44
Gift Baskets ... 48
Custom Baskets ... 52

CHAPTER THREE

Special Occasion Baskets ... 96

Sources ... 126   Index ... 127

INTRODUCTION

The basket, that simple container made of interwoven strips of wood, twigs, or rushes, has always held a special place in my memories. That classic shape and form has always been familiar, always been friendly. I remember my childhood excitement when I finally found that elusive Easter basket. It was carefully decorated with colored paper and ribbons and always overflowing with painted eggs and chocolate rabbits. And I have memories of other baskets. My grandmother had a fine old Chinese sewing basket with glass beads and old coins attached to the top; my mother's sewing basket was square and lined with cloth; and I don't know how many hours I spent practicing my hook shot in the laundry basket. Later in life I spent just as many hours outside with my garden basket in hand. Each basket had a function, and when not in use it was stored in the garage or the basement.

There were a few baskets, however, that were not used for specific functions, but were placed within the home as deco-

ration. There was a pretty basket with a tall handle that always held summer flowers, and a small basket made by a Native American that held a special place on the mantle. I appreciated these baskets in a very different way than, say, the laundry basket, which was purchased from the hardware store. Despite the fact that the laundry basket had also been made by hand, the other baskets, the little Native American one especially, had a greater link to the legacy of the basket-making craftsman.

The tradition of basket making is one of the oldest known to man, and one that continues today with ancient methods and materials. The Native American basket, although originally made to serve some functional purpose, took on an artistic significance because of its beautiful workmanship and attention to detail. Unlike purely *functional basket forms, such as the laundry basket, this small work of art retained an elevated place within the household.*

For a while, the introduction of plastic as a replacement for handmade baskets seemed to threaten the traditional practices of the basket trade. Today, however, basket makers and buyers have returned to the earlier forms of the craft and reassessed their values, not necessarily in functional terms, but in terms of the basket's aesthetic integrity. The world of basketry has opened up and become an integrated part of our cultural style. Interior designers freely employ baskets as decorative accents. Collectors prize them as historical documents of past civilizations. Shops throughout the world overflow with baskets of every size, shape, and purpose. In modern society, the once purely functional basket has been given a new prominence and independence. No longer are baskets simply used for their traditional functions, they have now become elevated to objects of art. What was once assigned shelf space in the basement, attic or even garage, has now been dusted off and given a fresh new life.

For centuries people in every culture, from the most simple to the most sophisticated, have used baskets. Made primarily for gathering or for storage, early baskets were discarded and replaced after they wore out or became damaged. Replacement was a matter of function. A similar basket took the place of the old one, and developing new aesthetics didn't play a part in the process. Guilds of craftsmen made the baskets used by early cultures. They passed down their methods and styles of basket making from one generation to another. The industry was small and well defined, using uniform designs and methods of production. Today in many parts of the world, craftsmen still construct the same style baskets that served their culture for thousands of years. The size, proportion, and other identifiable qualities of these baskets, such as the overall woven pattern and what components are stained with dyes, have been well established by the rhythm of time.

While baskets have undergone somewhat of an aesthetic revolution over the past several years, their functional use has not fallen completely to the wayside. In fact, baskets have taken on some very original uses. They not only continue to hold farm produce in country stands, but now also hold socks, cosmetics, cassette tapes, and any number of other household items.

Modern basket makers, unlike their ancient predecessors, are much more adventurous in the designs and colors they choose for even the most functional basket. Still, this doesn't mean that the basket industry has made a complete turn for the new. Old baskets, with their traditional weavings and ancient patina, have enjoyed a rebirth of interest and use. Truly, it is the old baskets that retain the greatest presence and value.

This book of baskets is designed to spark the imagination and whet the appetite for artistic adventure, as well as in-

struct the reader how to make, customize, and alter a wide variety of beautiful baskets. Included are some baskets made from scratch and others made unique through a variety of decorating techniques. There are over forty different approaches to creating unusual and personal baskets, many with clear step-by-step instructions. In this book I cover painting and stenciling techniques, as well as the use of cloth and even buttons to transform a charming flea market find into a useful sewing container or a beautiful decoration for your home. Learn how to plant a summer herb garden in a basket or how to make your child happy with his or her own animal basket made from a few pieces of wood and a stack of nesting baskets. Baskets are also a wonderful gift idea. There is nothing more satisfying than creating a beautiful and personal gift for someone special. With this book I invite you to explore the artistic world of basketry. Reap its benefits, and enjoy the stunning results.

Beautiful Baskets from Scratch

There is nothing more satisfying than the act of creating—developing a concept and then realizing that concept by manipulating raw materials into a final, original form. This creative process is at the heart of making baskets from scratch. In this chapter, I will discuss the basic techniques for making baskets from scratch. Here you will learn how to weave, paint, glue, and knot a wide range of materials in order to make a variety of basket forms. Once you have finished this chapter, mix, adjust, and experiment with these techniques to develop your own unique creations. The possibilities are endless.

BASIC TOOLS AND MATERIALS

In beginning any creative project, it is essential to have an accessible work area that is equipped with the proper tools and materials. Now, this doesn't mean you have to add an extension to your house or convert the garage into a work shop; it simply suggests that providing the best possible work area and having the required tools and materials before you begin a basket project will make the actual process much more enjoyable and satisfying.

The two essentials for any practical work area are space and light. You need enough room to spread out your work and enough light to see exactly what you are doing. If a working space is too small it will restrict your movements while making the basket, and if it is too dark—especially when painting or sewing—the final outcome may be drastically different from what you had expected. I try to assess any specific needs prior to beginning a project then choose the kind of space that will best aid me in constructing the basket. I usually work indoors in my studio; however, I have worked outside on a picnic table when lighting and the materials have permitted it. There is nothing wrong with the kitchen floor or the utility table when a need for mobility and flexibility outweigh a permanent work space. Still, no matter where you work, you must have a good source of light. If you are weaving a basket from a kit, or painting a design on another, the outcome of each effort you make should not be a disappointing surprise because your working space or light conditions weren't their best. I suggest clip-on lights as a supplementary source of light. They cast a direct and flexible beam.

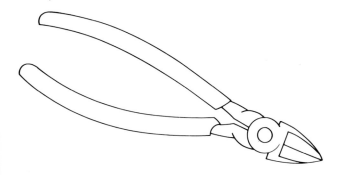

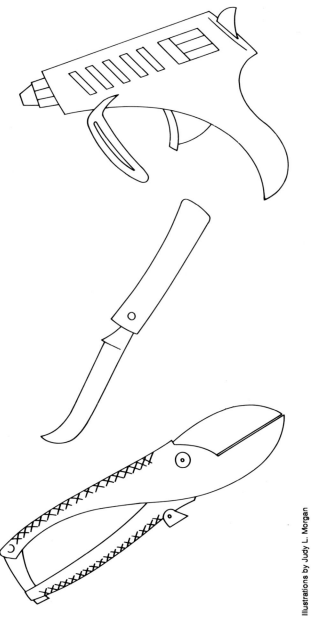

Next to sufficient space and light, the most important aspect of a good work area is a sturdy working surface. There is nothing worse than having a wiggling table under your project when you are attempting a particularly delicate procedure. The surface should also be at a comfortable height for you to work—either standing or sitting, depending on your preference. By having the proper height adjustment you will avoid hours of debilitating back pain.

Having the basic tools and materials on hand will help you to streamline your work and free up your time for the maximum creative work. It is essential to have a pair of gardening clippers, wire cutters, and regular scissors on hand. A pocket knife is also a handy tool for a variety of cutting, scraping, and prying jobs—especially when you are out looking for the perfect dried flower or grape vine. Other helpful tools include a claw hammer, a screwdriver, a pair of needle nose pliers, an array of paint brushes, and some sandpaper. In many cases, the tools you require will depend on the type of basket you in-

Illustrations by Judy L. Morgan

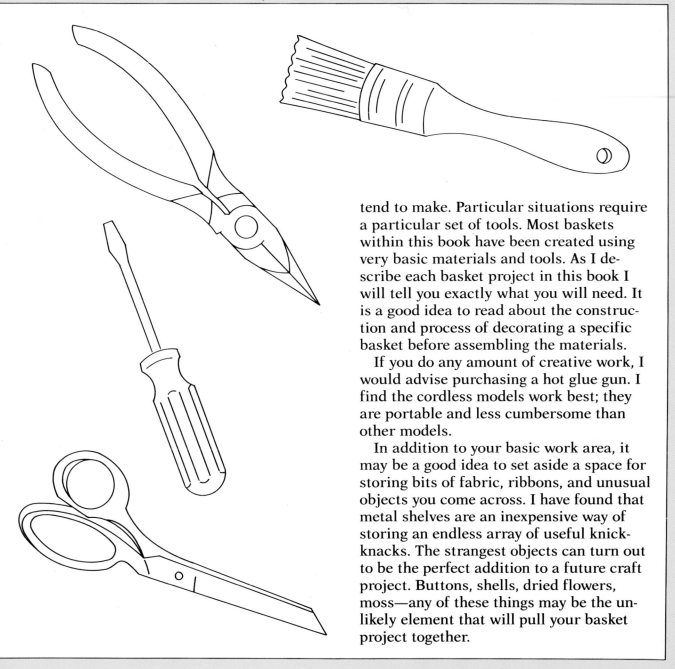

tend to make. Particular situations require a particular set of tools. Most baskets within this book have been created using very basic materials and tools. As I describe each basket project in this book I will tell you exactly what you will need. It is a good idea to read about the construction and process of decorating a specific basket before assembling the materials.

If you do any amount of creative work, I would advise purchasing a hot glue gun. I find the cordless models work best; they are portable and less cumbersome than other models.

In addition to your basic work area, it may be a good idea to set aside a space for storing bits of fabric, ribbons, and unusual objects you come across. I have found that metal shelves are an inexpensive way of storing an endless array of useful knick-knacks. The strangest objects can turn out to be the perfect addition to a future craft project. Buttons, shells, dried flowers, moss—any of these things may be the unlikely element that will pull your basket project together.

DEVELOPING A PLAN

When making a basket from scratch, it is important to familiarize yourself with baskets that have a similar feel. Look at a variety of baskets. Hold them. Become familiar with the basket form. Your imagination will be sparked by the wide variety of baskets that can be found in craft stores, in the homes of friends, and on the pages of your favorite magazines.

As with any craft project, planning is very important. Before you start, you need at least a general idea of what size and proportion you want the finished product to be. Given the creative process, however, more times than not, the finished product will usually vary quite a bit from the original concept. But if you begin without a general idea of what you hope to accomplish, your efforts and materials most likely will go to waste.

When you begin weaving a basket by hand, it is helpful to have a point of reference to use as a guide. Whether you're working from an existing basket that may be lying around the house, a photograph, or a rough sketch that you've drawn up on your own, you will find that having some sort of coherent plan is invaluable. Based on my own experience I have found that it is best to have an actual basket in front of you to hold and examine. In this way you can see just how the basket is constructed. It is not always possible to find exactly what you are looking for, but with so many

basket types and styles available, you should not have too much trouble finding something similar to what you want your basket to look like.

Having a plan and a reference will actually provide you with a great deal of flexibility. When creating anything from scratch, you must realize that often the materials used will influence the process and the final result. By developing a flexible outlook and an understanding of the process and the materials you are using, you will be able to avoid a great deal of frustration. This is not to say, however, that the materials and the process should dictate the design concept or even the approach you take to the project. It is simply a reminder that one material will operate differently from another, and this will ultimately affect the appearance of your finished basket.

BASKETRY KITS

There are a number of kits available in a number of different basket shapes. These can be purchased at craft stores or through mail order (see page 126 for a list of Sources). These kits are a wonderful way for the novice basket maker to begin. They'll give you an immediate point of reference as you proceed through each step. Both the finished basket and the kit instructions will then help you make similar baskets from scratch. These kits include clear, step-by-step instructions as well as all the materials you will need to complete the specific basket. Basket kits provide a solid foundation from which to explore different combinations of techniques and materials, so you can make your own, very personalized basket.

COIL BASKETS

The coil method is one of the oldest and most consistent methods of basket making. They are wrapped from a long length of rope that is fastened with strips of cloth, raffia, or, more traditionally, grass. The technique and materials have evolved over the years, but the entire process remains simple and very satisfying.

The basic materials needed for creating a coil basket are a length of clothesline or other similar rope; a large-eyed needle (I prefer a rug needle); and some material to wrap the rope with, such as long, one-inch strips of fabric. Cut or tear an old sheet, a two- or three-yard piece of fabric for the one-inch strips.

Once you have prepared plenty of fabric, thread the first piece through the needle, passing it just a few inches through the eye. Then take the end of the rope in your left hand and wrap it a few times with the strip of fabric. To do this, simply lay the loose end of the fabric strip onto the rope about an inch and a half from the rope tip. Then wrap the fabric around, towards the tip, in an overlapping manner until the rope end is covered. This process locks the fabric onto the rope and gives you a clean start to your basket.

The whole procedure in constructing a coil basket is to coil the rope around itself, while continually securing it with the fabric. To begin, turn the wrapped end of the rope into itself. Then, with the threaded

needle, put a stitch into the fabric on the wrapped end. This locks the fabric and allows you to move forward.

The rule for the winding rhythm is to wrap the rope with four loops, and then secure it by putting a stitch through the wrapped rope on the inside coil. Make four more wraps, coil the freshly wrapped rope and secure it with another stitch. By continuing the four wraps and then a stitch pattern, and then continually coiling the rope, a basket form will take shape. This process creates a firm basket with a consistent pattern of binding and will allow you to make a number of basic, flat and bowl-shaped basket forms.

Having long lengths of striped fabric allows a certain amount of weaving freedom before it is time to tie on another strip. To give the basket a continuous even surface on the outside, join the two pieces of fabric so that the knot appears in the inner side of the basket, leaving the outer surface free from any obvious mechanics. When you are ready to end the basket, simply cut the rope, allowing two inches for wrapping, and secure it into the existing rim of the basket with a few stitches.

The traditional coiled baskets on these pages are all from South Asia. They represent how grass and fibers can be used in this method of construction. Raffia can be bought pre-packaged at craft stores and flower shops. Threading single lengths of either natural or colored raffia, and following the procedure described for coil construction makes a fine looking basket.

VINE BASKETS

Much of the pleasure I experience when making baskets comes from the repetitive rhythm that accompanies the process. Most basket-making processes are designed to create an even, uniform surface, making repetition a must. Vine baskets, on the other hand, require a much more spontaneous method that requires more imagination and immediate decision making. This spontaneity offers a creative freedom that can be very rewarding.

Although a characteristic of a good vine is a very homemade, rustic look, it is still important, as with any basket, to have a rough idea of the basic size or shape you want to end up with. The plan should be flexible in order to allow the natural shapes of the vines to determine and

emerge into the final look of the basket.

The most important piece of equipment for making a vine basket is a good pair of heavy-duty garden clippers. These are used to trim the vines to size, or, if you are more ambitious, to gather your own vines. I think there are few things more satisfying than hiking through the woods gathering vines (grapevines and wisteria work the best) and then using the vines to make a beautiful basket. If you do choose to gather your own vines, look up in trees for wild, long single vines that can be easily pulled down. If you are not so ambitious, a wide variety of natural and dried vines are available at any craft or flower store.

After you've made a basic plan, the first step is to separate and group the vines ac-

cording to their length and width. This will help ensure an even flow from one vine to the next when winding the basket. Start with a good sturdy vine and bend it into a circle, passing the vine over and under itself to lock in the shape. Then shift directions and create another circular form laying it perpendicular to the original. These two circles will form the base and the handle of the finished basket, thus determining the basket's final dimensions. The larger the circle, the wider or deeper the basket and the higher the handle.

The fun starts when you take the wisteria, or any other manageable vine, and weave the body of the basket. Start in the middle of the perpendicular circles and weave the first vine over and under, over and under in a circular motion around the base. How tightly you wrap the vine will determine how dense you want the finished basket to be. Gradually draw the outer vine wraps in tighter to form a basket shape. As you establish the proportions, pass the vine over and under itself to lock it into the desired shape. When you have the basic form completed, go back and fill in the basket with thinner vines until you achieve the desired shape and density. What you are doing is filling in space with the vine. If you want to fill out a particular area, simply add more vines to fill in the blanks.

After the form is completed, secure the ends by either tucking them in, for a neater, more unified look, or leaving them dangling for a wild, unkempt look.

LOG CABIN BASKETS

While working with vine is imaginative and improvisational, making a log cabin is much more exacting. It also requires additional tools and materials. These include a good saw and hammer, nails (I recommend paneling nails, as they tend not to pull out of the wood), a measuring tape, and a pair of garden clippers.

Precut all of the twigs you will be using so that construction can be completed without unnecessary interruptions. I find that twigs, as opposed to dowels or saw cut lumber, often have a mind of their own and don't always do exactly what I want. I usually give in, and let the twigs' natural configuration influence the shape of the

basket. Just as with the vine baskets, no two twig baskets are quite alike. Although all log cabin baskets have a similar size and structure, the unpredictability of the materials gives each basket a distinct personality and character.

This method of basket making is by far the easiest and the most enjoyable. It gives the basket maker the control of choosing the materials through all stages of construction for any type of basket.

I begin from the bottom and work up to the top and if I'm including a handle, I attach it last. Try adding two side handles as a variation. In this way the shape of the basket becomes elongated visually and may fit your needs better. There are a number of variations of this log cabin method of construction. For example, by incorporating some natural vines with the twigs you'll achieve some interesting results. You can also bend twigs, but you must be careful not to snap them or use them in such a way as to put too much stress on the bend. Little twig baskets with slat twig bottoms are great for holding plants as well as acting as containers for a number of other materials. Use them on your picnic table for serving cheese, or for condiments for the barbecue. Add a waterproof container then fill it with fresh flowers for a centerpiece, or add pine cones, shells, or fresh greens and give the basket a home within your home. The shape is a versatile one and the simple construction allows you complete liberty in deciding for yourself.

BARK CONE BASKETS

During a recent winter storm, a few birch trees fell to the weather. It seemed wise to cut them up and retain them for future use. The cone shaped basket has been made simply by using some bark from one of the trees. I have patterned the construction of this decorative basket from the cylindrical basket of bark. The cylindrical basket was purchased and is widely available in better shops. You will need very few materials to reproduce a bark basket.

It should be said here that bark may easily be substituted for other materials such as paper, light cardboard, or bark cloth. If you do use bark, or something that is basically brittle when dry, first soak the substance. I left the piece of bark in warm water for about a half hour, while I prepared the other materials. Bark cuts easily with garden clippers, as does the vine used here for the handle. I used the wide-eyed needle that had been the main tool in constructing the coiled-rope basket for sewing the vine to the bark. Raffia was the thread I chose. Once the bark was flexible, I made a simple cone allowing the V-top to flair out in width. Using a piece of grapevine, cut with my garden clippers, I simply inserted the vine through the two layers of the bark. I passed the vine through the bark from the inside to the outer surface at the top bark cone. That was the only means of attaching the two surfaces together. Attaching the handle was equally easy. Using the raffia threaded through the needle, I sewed an "X" over the vine, binding it to the bark. Two points of attachment would work equally well. Using the garden clippers again, I straightened the bottom of the basket by trimming it and gently rolled the edge of the top for interest. It would be very easy to cut a circle for the bottom and sew it to the body of the basket by using the raffia and needle. A vine rim lining the top and bottom, which adds a lovely little lip to the top and bottom of the basket, was also added. Vine assists in strengthening and decorating the structure.

WIRE PLANTING BASKETS

Wire baskets are widely available in a number of sizes at garden shops, florists, and craft stores. These baskets can be customized and used as planting baskets. The beauty of a planting basket is that it can be used in any season, either outdoors in the summer, or indoors in the cold months of winter. The strawberry plant basket planter was constructed using peat moss and soil, and then filled with four strawberry plants.

To make a planting basket, soak peat moss in water for an hour, or until it is saturated. Squeeze the excess water from the peat and line the basket with it. Be sure the basket is fully lined with the peat in order to avoid leaks. The peat keeps dirt and excess water from running out of the basket and allows the plant to breathe.

Finally, pour a little soil into the basket, place the strawberry plants on top, and then cover their roots with more soil, gently patting it down to make it firm but not too compressed. It is important to water the plant now to test the peat moss for leaks. If it does, remember the little Dutch boy who used his finger to plug the hole in the dike and wedge an additional clump of peat moss into the leak.

The final result is a small, portable strawberry garden. When the plants are full of blossoms or ready to harvest, this basket makes a beautiful center piece for a dinner party. It also provides a wonderful opportunity for children to see plants develop through their growing cycle.

Ivy also works very well in a wire planting basket. A lush ivy basket is at home in a number of environments, both formal and informal, indoors and out. English ivy is available through all florists and nurseries, and requires minimal upkeep. Try a variegated ivy plant and plant a couple of African violets in the center of the soil. The color will complement the white and green pattern of the ivy. Ivy will attach itself to the peat moss and simply cover the entire basket in a very delightful way.

Try making a basket. It can bring you a great amount of pleasure and satisfaction. Your efforts will add personality to your home. Place your handmade baskets among your other decorative objects. Your efforts will bring to your home a part of your personality. Use your baskets. Bring them to the table filled with flowers or food. Make them part of your daily life and routine. Tackle a second basket, buy a kit, or make one from scratch. Do it for yourself. If you run into difficulty ask for assistance. Someone will help. I suggest you inquire at your craft shop, for many offer classes and will be able to answer your questions. The most important thing is to do, and to enjoy.

Customized Store-Bought Baskets

Not everyone who appreciates the true beauty and workmanship of a fine basket necessarily wants to make one from scratch. The wide availability of quality baskets makes constructing one from scratch almost obsolete for those people who lack the time and the patience. Yet, there are countless ways to customize even the most generic basket in order to give it a personality of its own.

This chapter provides you with a number of ideas and how-to instructions for antiquing baskets, adding personal touches to your favorite old baskets or newly purchased ones, customizing a basket for a particular function, and using baskets in new and interesting ways.

LIVING BASKETS

Earlier I discussed the procedure for filling a wire basket with peat moss and planting in it to create a living basket. This represents just one way of creating a living basket. Another way is to use a basket that is less porous in structure than wire, such as one made of vine or wicker. When using an open weave basket, such as I did for this herb garden planter it is very important to protect the basket itself from the excess moisture that normally builds up in the soil. First line the interior of the basket with heavy plastic. Black plastic works best as it will be less visible if there are any slight openings in the basket weave. Next, fill the basket with a rich mixture of soil. Check with your local garden center and make sure the soil is properly balanced for the plants you intend to plant. Place the plants in the soil in a pleasing arrangement that will not interfere with their growth. Once planted, give the plants a good watering and place the basket outside for some direct sunlight. I like to keep this herb basket within easy reach of my kitchen door so that I can snip off fresh herbs as I need them. The advantage of a living basket is that you can move it around for the best light and bring it inside when cool weather doesn't permit growing plants outside.

Another method for creating a living basket is to simply place a potted plant inside it, instead of planting directly into the bas-

ket. Baskets are a natural for holding potted plants of any size or form. Before placing the potted plant into the basket (see the yellow mums in the ivory-washed basket on page 44), first surround the pot with a black plastic liner to protect not only the basket, but also the surface that the basket rests upon. Plastic liners come in a number of sizes to fit virtually any pot. This precaution provides insurance against occasional overwatering. I choose plastic over the traditional clay saucer because clay, by its porous nature, can emit moisture. If the top of the pot is visible inside the basket, add some Spanish moss to cover the edge.

ANTIQUING A BASKET

Often I retain the natural finish of my baskets, but sometimes they need a wash of color to help them work within the surroundings of a specific room. Antiquing, the process of washing a hint of color onto a basket, is a refreshingly simple way to breathe new life into an old basket or to enhance the beauty of a store-bought one.

To antique a basket you will need: 1) a light, natural-toned basket; 2) a sponge and a two-inch paint brush; 3) your choice of color in acrylic paint (blue and brown work best for an antique look); 4) plenty of newspapers and clean cloth rags; and 5) a good clear working surface (an outdoor picnic table is ideal). Remember, the point here is not to fully paint the basket, but to provide a hint of color that appears to have worn off the basket with time.

Working on one side of the basket at a time, brush the color on and into the fibers of the basket weave. Make sure you really cover all surfaces of the woven pattern. Allow the paint to become absorbed, but not totally dry. Because you are using acrylic-based paints that are water soluble, they are easy to manipulate. Now, use the sponge to rub off the paint that has been allowed to set on the basket. If the paint is too dry, moisten the sponge and gently wipe the painted surface, lifting the color off. With practice this becomes a very easy and natural procedure. When one side of your basket is complete, move onto the next side, repeat the process, being careful to keep the color balanced on all sides of the basket.

This process also works well if you first paint the basket with a base of solid color. When it's completely dry, add a wash of a second color and antique it over the first using the method I outlined above.

Paint applied to a basket has its merits. It offers a way in which a familiar form takes on a new life. Some argue that you should leave well enough alone, while others enthusiastically support the theory that adding fresh color and decoration enhances and enriches the basket.

The dark-stained, split-wood picnic basket is available with either a natural finish or a dark stain. I chose a darker, stained basket with the idea of adding deep, rich tones of muted colors that would blend with and compliment the overall tonality of the stained basket. It seemed appropriate not to give the basket a total covering of color, as was done in the gift basket on page 118 (every slat of the woven construction was colored a separate shade of red). I thought it better to accent the woven rhythms of the picnic basket construction.

To do this I chose a palette of five colors and randomly applied them to the four sides of the basket, keeping the paint strokes fluid and graceful. The top of the basket was constructed with individual wooden slats, so I accented each of these with an individual color. In turn, I painted the handles and rim of the basket with a deep barn red.

The paint application accents the structural character of this basket, while maintaining the original integrity of the stained surface. In many ways, it is the perfect basket to take on an autumn picnic. The shape of any individual basket usually determines what paint treatment would work best on it.

GIFT BASKETS

When I found this pleasantly detailed, peach-colored, woven basket my immediate impulse was to use it as gift container. The basket functions as a box holding an additional gift inside. In essence, two gifts are given. To wrap the basket, I simply added a wide lace ribbon and a cluster of flowers—leaving as much of the basket exposed as possible.

A gift basket is a special second present that reflects your degree of caring and attention to detail. There are many other baskets throughout this book that would make wonderful gift containers. As you

flip through these pages, keep an eye out for innovative ways to present that perfect gift. Brightly colored nested baskets take on a totally new and humorous character when given a coat of bright paint and adorned with multicolored pom poms (page 85). What child wouldn't enjoy having birthday gifts tucked within the playful "boxes" seen on (page 86). For Christmastime gifts, paint the basket shades of holiday colors and add white pom poms to simulate snow. Or stripe the basket with masking tape and add red, white, and green pom poms.

The finest aspect of these gift baskets is that you make the most simple process, that of gift giving, one of excitement and adventure. You will be remembered for your thoughtfulness long after the time of giving. That in itself will make the time spent on decorating your basket "gift box" rewarding.

Giving a basket need not be expensive for there are tremendous values within the price brackets of baskets. And there's no reason why one has to give a new basket; especially if you already have some at home that don't seem to fit your own needs. How about refurbishing one with a fresh wash of color as previously described? Or take a bargain basket purchased from a country flea market or a secondhand shop and repaint it, as was done with this sewing basket.

This antique sewing basket was in need of some repairs, which did not entail any great skill or time. Once the repairs were completed, I gave the whole basket a fresh coat of black paint, using a spray can. When the basket was thoroughly dry, I sewed multi-colored buttons of various sizes over the top and sides of the basket. This button treatment gave the basket an additional touch of fun and character. A new tassel was switched to the center of the lid to complete the renovation of my flea market find. By adding a ribbon and a name tag this once dilapidated sewing basket was transformed into a delightful, color-filled gift basket.

CUSTOM BASKETS

The ideas presented in this book are designed to spur the imagination and to provide basic techniques for you to use as a foundation to further explore your own creativity. By using these ideas and adding ideas of your own you should be well on your way to developing a vast array of personalized custom baskets.

I customized these baskets with romantic colors and flowered patterns for use as a picnic basket, but that was a choice made from many possibilities. Why not line the basket with a bright child's fabric and use it as a toy box? Or use holiday fabrics to make a basket to hold cards, or special holiday foods.

Fabric-Lined Picnic Basket

This picnic basket was a two-part project. Not only did I trim the basket with cut-flower fabric, but I also lined the interior with the same fabric. To make the lining you will need a piece of fabric long and wide enough to accommodate the container's proportions—a yard of 54-inch wide material was sufficient for this project. In addition, you will need fabric scissors, matching thread, velcro strips, a bottle of white glue, a paint brush or a hot glue gun, a sewing machine (although you can sew the lining by hand), tissue or newsprint paper, and a reliable tape measure.

First, trace the bottom of your basket onto the tracing paper. Then cut out the tracing, lay the cut shape inside the basket, and correct and adjust the paper by trimming it where needed, until it fits comfortably inside. Next, measure the interior dimension of the basket's height and length. When measuring the dimensions on the fabric allow a half inch extra for all seams. Then cut the fabric. Cut another strip of fabric for a ruffle, keeping your proportions compatible to the basket's shape and size. To do this double the width of the basket and add on an additional inch for the seams. For this picnic basket, a three-inch ruffle was used. Hand baste the ruffle, gathering it to fit the lip of the basket. Pin the ruffle to the lining fabric and machine stitch all the seams. Attach a length of velcro to the edge of the inside of the basket with a hot glue gun, or with tacky white glue and allow it to dry. Next, attach the corresponding length of the velcro by machine to the reverse side of the basket lining and then the lining to the basket.

Next, cut individual flowers or flower clusters out of the remaining fabric, then apply the flowers to the basket with the hot glue gun or thick white glue. Be sure to securely adhere the edges of the flowers to the outer basket surface. Continue this process until you have covered the outer basket with a pleasant arrangement of flowers. These flowers can form any number of configurations, depending on your aesthetic judgement as well as on the basic shape of the basket. If you have material

left, you may wish to make a few napkins or to cut a square to use as a table or ground cover.

Ideas for customizing baskets for particular uses are endless. Line a basket with a baby print and fill the basket with baby supplies to be used on the changing table. Or line a basket with a certain design and paint matching designs on the basket itself. Combining projects and techniques simply makes your customized basket more distinctive and allows you to use your talents in the best ways.

Stone-Finish Tray Baskets

One of the pleasures of basketry is exploring the market place for new products and then figuring out innovative ways to use them. Recently I came across a kit for painting a stone-like finish on any surface. These kits are widely available in craft stores and come in a variety of finishes, including marble, brick, and wood. I applied this unique finish to two tray baskets and a plant container. The process is so straightforward and simple that anyone can enjoy stunning results in a matter of a few minutes. The kit contains two cans of spray—the first an acrylic sealer to protect the surface from moisture, the second a stone fleck paint. By following directions, the tray and plant baskets were instantly transformed into new, innovative and exciting works of art.

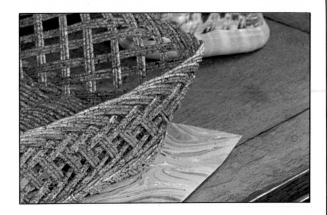

It is important to realize that you can create unique basket decorations with any number and combination of materials. Some processes are more complicated than others, and some take a little practice to master. But the range of possibilities is endless and the variations lead to your own invention. Each variation produces new visual possibilities.

Spray-Paint Ribbon Basket

The basket holding a swan topiary (pages 56, 57) uses a spray paint finish and a creative twist ribbon purposely set off center. The bow was separately attached to the basket with a hot glue gun. The basket and bow were then sprayed with flat white paint, purposely leaving some of the under color of the paper ribbon and the basket's natural finish exposed. The effect is a softer overall feeling than that of a totally opaque white basket.

Spray-Paint Doily Basket

With every material, comes multiple possibilities for creative decoration. Using spray paints can produce a soft and delicate surface, one that has a definite difference from that of a brush painted surface. This basket was completely painted with spray paints. I first gave the basket an overall coat of white paint. When that had sufficiently dried, I attached a paper doily to the top edges of the basket with a clothes pin. I then sprayed teal and larkspur blue paint on the body of the basket. The spray paint penetrated through the perforated edge of the doily and marked the basket with a soft duplication of the doily pattern. The random mixture of the two colors of bluish paint softened the whole feeling of the basket surface. This simple and direct process clearly demonstrates how easy it is to take the most common of objects on hand and use them creatively. A similar effect can be achieved by stenciling the doily pattern onto the basket with a sponge and diluted acrylic paint.

Moss-Covered Mushroom Basket

This moss-covered mushroom basket is a very quick and easy project that uses the versatile hot glue gun. Sheets of dried moss and mushroom-shaped baskets are available through your local florist or craft store. Of course, you can add satin ribbon, bits of dried flowers, or many other materials to alter this design, or you can keep the basket plain. I lined the basket with plastic pot saucers and placed three pots of spring violas inside. This idea can easily be finessed with any flower available during any season.

Dried moss will fade into a less attractive shade of brownish green if exposed to direct sunlight for prolonged periods of time. To return the dried moss to a more lively green, simply take a spray bottle and fill it with water. Add a few drops of green food coloring. The amount of coloring needed will depend on just how failed the moss has become. Lightly spray the mixture over the faded moss and it will take on a healthy-looking green color.

By adding other types of moss or fungi to the sheet moss with the hot glue gun you can create variations on this basket-making idea. The additional moss adds an interesting texture to the basket that keeps with the overall mushroom theme.

Harvest Basket

The harvest basket is a true work of beauty that represents both the labors of the gardener and the basket maker. This harvest basket contains a harvest of late summer flowers (coxcomb, straw flowers, rose hips, yarrow, and statice). I first enhanced the handle and rim of the basket with a freshly picked grapevine, which still held on to some of its leaves. To secure the vines to the basket, simply interlock the ends of the vines together. For extra safety use a few lengths of florist wire. Twist the wire together and cut off the remaining ends. When adding the dried elements to the basket remember to cover any wire with a little moss or a dried flower. When you feel you have decorated the handle and rim of the basket sufficiently with the fresh grapevines, begin to hot glue your selection of dried flowers. It is important to have all the materials at hand before starting the basket. I find the best way to prepare for a hot glue project is to work on a large clear surface, near an electrical outlet, and with good light.

Begin by attaching like elements one at a time, placing them around the rim and on the handle in a rhythmic pattern. This establishes the design as well as the dominant flow of color. Next, slowly fill in the design by using additional colors and textures chosen from the other dried materials. Continue to apply dried flowers. If you

like, add a tuft of moss, a pine cone, or berry to finish the work. Try to avoid adding any type of stationary focal point and instead strive for a continuous visual flow of random clusters, each holding individual interest. Building up these areas of interest depends on the use of materials that have color variations as well as scale differences. The changing texture of the elements adds to the overall spirit and effect of the composition.

When deciding what materials to use, remember to select elements that work well together. If you use dried pods and flowers, consider the scale and the overall range of color of the elements. Unify the composition with similar materials that will create a feeling of unity. Experiment with your materials and always have some extras available. It's difficult to predetermine just how much of any single material you will need and it is very frustrating to run out in the middle of a project. You can always use extra flowers or pods on a smaller basket and pass it along to someone as a gift.

Instead of using dried garden flowers, you may want to cover your basket with silk flowers or blossoms made from corn husks. Try using a creatively twisted ribbon instead of the natural grapevines. Experimenting is half the fun, and with your hot glue gun, the work is enjoyable.

Seashell Basket

The seashell basket is a variation on the dried flower basket treatment. The shell arrangement is more controlled and clustered to one side of the basket than the harvest basket. The handle of the former is wrapped with satin ribbon. Two bows of the same ribbon have been incorporated into the design. Star fish, shells, and coral are the elements of the major part of this composition. The unifying base is a foundation of Spanish moss that was first glued to the rim and the side of the basket. I laid out all the shells that I had to work with first so I could select which shells would be placed where. When I felt the composition was right, I glued down the pieces. Scale and color were prime considerations. It is the relationship of one object to the next that creates the natural visual order and rhythm of any composition. I wanted the shell arrangement to retain a fluid character.

Earlier in the summer I had dried some daisies and black-eyed Susans that I harvested from a nearby field. I added them to the shell basket because of their color and their fresh summer feeling. These flowers seemed appropriate for the shells and the overall composition. Sometimes a shell may not hold to the basket as well as it should because of its natural contour, or its weight. If this happens, take a small, three-inch florist pick and hot glue it to the back side of the shell, leaving a good portion of the pick extending below the shell. Simply wedge the pick into the weave of the basket and cover it with some moss or another shell. It is important to remember that when working with a three-dimensional composition you must consider the inside of the arrangement as well as the outside. If the finished product will be seen from all directions, make sure you have addressed each visual area.

Stenciled Pie Basket

At times the most simple techniques can produce the most satisfying outcome. A fresh coat of paint will refurbish an old basket and bring it back to new life. As with the old sewing basket, simple paint and colorful buttons can give a once worn basket a whole new character. Here, a pie basket has been decorated a number of ways. The basket itself had been natural, free from stain, and thus receptive to color.

I painted each of the vertical ribs of the basket a deep, rich green. I then sponged the horizontal slats with the same green paint. When sponging slats, use a small sponge approximately the same size as the surface you are painting to achieve the greatest possible control. You can easily cut a kitchen sponge with an everyday pair of scissors. Then simply mix your acrylic paint and pat the sponge into it a few times, making sure that the whole surface of the sponge has been covered with pigment. For best results, blot the sponge onto a paper towel to get rid of the excess paint. To apply the paint to the basket surface, gently press the sponge against the basket and release. If you wish to deepen the color or alter the density, repeat the procedure. It is a good idea to experiment on another surface before working on the basket. Using the same green paint and a brush, paint the top of the lid with a solid even coat of color. In this example, I painted the top band and the handle of the basket with a contrasting, yet complimentary color to accentuate the basket's construction. The next step is to stencil the lid of the basket. To do this you will need a mat or razor knife, a sheet of stencil paper, a pencil, a few sheets of tracing paper, and, of course, a few tubes of acrylic paint. Begin planning the stencil design by first tracing the shape of the lid onto the tracing paper. If the design repeats itself, then divide the surface of the lid into quarters or thirds. This basket lid was designed in quarters with a bow inserted into the com-

position. Select one segment of the design and trace it onto another sheet of paper and retrace it until it fills the entire area. In this case four times. That way you see how the whole composition will look. After this is done you can alter the arrangement to suit your specifications and aesthetic taste. The next step is to plan the color scheme and paint a version on paper to see how the finished product will look.

To cut the stencil, simply lay the stencil paper over a freshly drawn design and tape down both papers. Using your razor knife carefully cut out the areas that the paint will cover. Cut out the entire design before you begin applying the paint so that you won't have to worry about lining up one segment with another.

Once the stencil has been cut, transfer it to the lid of your pie basket and tape down the edges. Mix one color at a time and dab the stencil brush into the paint, blotting it a few times on a paper towel, before applying it to the lid. The technique for stenciling is to dab with the stencil brush in short rapid strikes, keeping the color within the boundaries of the cut shape. If needed, use masking tape to prevent unwanted color from accidentally hitting another color area. Remember to allow each color of paint to dry before applying another color. With acrylic paints the process is short; however, you can speed it up by using a hair dryer. After all the paint is dry, coat the entire basket with a layer of butcher's wax to seal the paint and protect it from damage.

Sponged Bushel Basket

The variations for painting and stenciling baskets are virtually endless. This painted and sponged bushel basket is a prime example of an attractive method for creating a country feeling on a common basket style. First, select the colors you wish to use for the stripes versus the color you will sponge over the entire basket. Next, measure the circumference of the basket and divide the number by four to determine the width of each stripe. Mark the basket with a pencil where each stripe begins. With a one-inch paint brush, paint each stripe, being careful to stay within the lines. Allow the basket to dry before sponging on the top design. Cut a kitchen sponge with ordinary scissors into a manageable but small square, and dip it into the paint. As stated before, make sure you blot the pigment prior to applying it onto the painted stripes. Begin at the top of the basket and repeat the pattern to the bottom of the striped portion of the basket. Allow some variations to occur as the process continues; however, make sure the color remains even in its intensity. Paint the rim and rib of the basket with one of the stripe colors to complete the project.

Patterned Quilt Basket

There are many basket surfaces that lend themselves to paint. A flatter tighter weave is easier than one made with a rounded fiber although both can be painted. The degree of detail you want is often determined by what style of basket you select. When reproducing the pattern of a favorite old quilt the best surface is one that in some way replicates the pattern of the textile. Because the quilt pattern is based on a grid, it is very easy to echo the pattern and scale by using a pre-cut chicken board plastic stencil.

To make this stencil, copy the basic pattern of the quilt onto a piece of tracing paper. Then color in the design with either colored pencil or paint. This gives you a good idea of how the final project will look. The basic pattern on this basket is small enough to repeat on both sides of the basket, with some room left for the handles. Paint on the base coat of the background color and, when that is completely dry, position the stencil and tape it down to the basket. I recommend that you use black paint to outline the basic design, as I did on this basket. Apply the black first to one side of the basket and when that is dry, reposition the stencil and apply the black design to the other side of the basket until the basic pattern is completed. Repeat the process, adding burnt orange and green paint in the same sequence as the first step. After the quilt pattern is finished, paint the inside of the basket with a coat of green paint. To finish the project, paint the handle and the top and bottom rim of the basket with burnt orange. This particular basket is now used as a magazine stand in my home next to the chair that holds the quilt it is based on.

The ability to reproduce your favorite quilt patterns or other textile motifs opens up a myriad of decorative possibilities within a home. Patchwork has such a bold design to it and repeats so naturally that it seems to be the perfect pattern for a flat weave basket. A stack of quilt-painted baskets can serve as a beautiful storage unit in a bedroom or small apartment.

Sewn-Pattern Basket

Although this next basket treatment is a departure from painting methods, the basic design is based on repetition as are those discussed earlier. A coil basket is the ideal base on which to add colorful sewn patterns with left over yarn. To do this, first sketch out a few pattern ideas on graph paper. Remember, that a well thought-out plan minimizes frustration and leads to a beautiful basket. Work out the proportions by taking measurements of the basket and then translate those measurements to graph paper scale.

If you are planning on using this basket for a particular room, choose a palette of colors that corresponds with the color theme of that room, or simply use any yarn at hand. To sew the yarn in place, you will need a large-eyed needle, one that is normally used for upholstery work. When you thread the needle, leave the ends of the yarn free; a knot would cause a lump on the inside of the basket. To secure the end on the basket, pull the thread almost through from the inside of the basket to the front, leaving one-half inch. Then lay that end against the rib of the basket and cover it with the subsequent stitches. When it is time to cut the yarn, take the needle, pass it through the wrapped yarn on the inside of the basket and cut it close. You will have locked the yarn into itself.

When you are exploring the market place for coiled baskets, examine each one

to see how it might serve your specific needs. There is quite a bit of variation within similar baskets. While this particular technique has a Southwest flavor, it isn't necessarily the only design concept that can be used on a coiled basket using a needle and remnants of yarn. Beautiful patches of color can be transformed into a fresh garden of flowers. Certain colors can be manipulated into block letters for a child's name. You could even sew on small toys for a child to enjoy. It's fun to add on objects that you make, buy, or simply have around the house.

Wooden Cut-Out Basket

Four wooden cut-out chickens are attached to the rim of the garden basket shown here. The bold paint job accentuates the clear, geometric quality of the basic weave. White and black dominate this palette and echo the colors of real chickens. The acid green of the trim gives the basket a visual punch, adding to the whimsical nature of the piece. To accentuate the boldness of the design, each color was given two coats so that the subtle fibers of the basket were lost within the paint. The cut-out chickens were added to the basket with small nails and wood glue. Each chicken was painted white or black and the reverse color was applied as feathers. To add the feathers, use a small watercolor brush and begin with a thin line. Then press down with the brush. The pressure will create the desired shape. Any number of delightful shapes could have been incorporated into this basket. More possibilities include little villages, ducks and geese, or scuttle dogs. Look in craft shops for many variations of pre-cut shapes. Let your imagination aid in your selection.

By changing the colors of a basket you can produce a totally different feeling and effect. Perhaps you could capture the four seasons with four of the same village shapes and trees, painted to correspond to summer, fall, winter, and spring. Attach a wooden shape to the handle and leave the basket rim plain. All sorts of variations are possible. The combinations are up to you.

Split-Wood Heart Basket

This beautiful split-wood round basket combines some of the techniques we have previously discussed. It was painted and adorned with pre-cut, painted hearts. The difference between this basket treatment and the one described above is that the paint has been sanded down to expose some of the basket's wood.

This process is simple. Paint the basket and the hearts. When everything is dry, use medium sandpaper and rough up the painted surface of the basket and the surface of hearts. Then hot glue the hearts to the basket.

Watermelon Basket

A nice variation on the wood cut-out theme is to fill a basket with wooden watermelon slices when it is not in use. I painted the exterior of this basket with green acrylic paint, using a standard one-inch paint brush. Then I sponged on lighter green areas and added white and green lines to approximate the texture and pattern of a watermelon. I painted the inside of the basket with a pinkish/red acrylic paint, and applied lighter tones of pink around the edge with a small water-color brush. I then randomly placed black seeds in the inside with a hot glue gun to make it appear as if the basket were an open watermelon. As with many of the basket treatments, the top rim and the handle were painted in a deeper color, to contrast with the rest of the basket, and extend the simple and eloquent construction of this traditional form.

My friend Stan cut the melon slices from logs, with his chain saw. I gave each slice a coat of white acrylic paint and then re-painted it in shades of red to purple. Give the basket as a gift, along with a few slices of real melon. It will be put to practical use in the summer garden, and then, during the winter, it will hold the colorful, wooden melon slices.

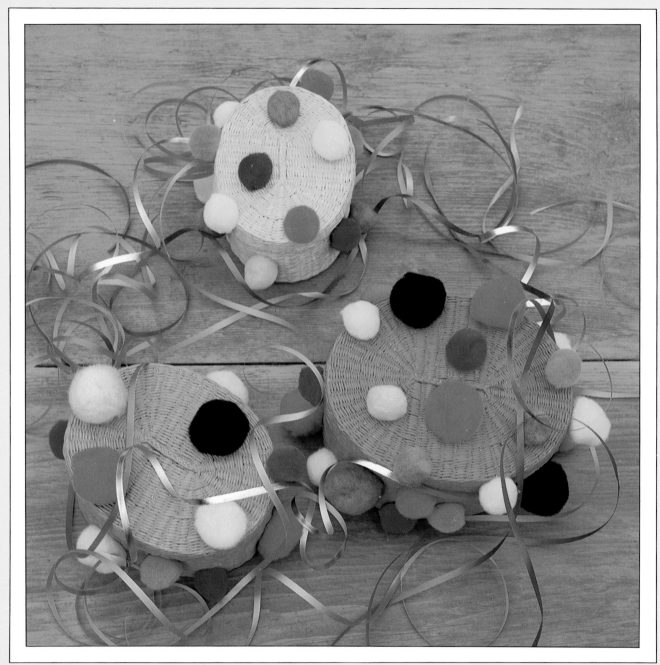

Pom Pom Nest Baskets

Parties seem like such a perfect time to pull out all the stops and be creative. Choosing gifts and wrapping presents can be so enjoyable. In many ways it's easier to personalize a gift basket for an adult, because their interests are more defined than a child's. But a child might enjoy a little basket that holds a gift and can be used as a container on its own. Every child needs a place to store those special items that he or she holds onto. This inexpensive nest of baskets was appropriate for the addition of brightly colored pom poms from the local craft store. Using your hot glue gun, the whole process can be done in a jiffy, with minimal cost. Pom poms come in a variety of sizes and colors, and can be combined with spangles and faux gems to make a basket that is the hit of the party.

To duplicate these funny, fancy boxes, simply look for a stack of baskets with lids. Buy bright acrylic paints, a one-half-inch paint brush, and a bag of assorted pom poms. Paint the boxes and, when the paint is completely dry, apply the pom poms with a hot glue gun. Add a polka dot ribbon or tie the packages up with curling ribbon. The spirit of the curling ribbon has the same amusing quality as does the party basket.

Fabric Gift Basket

Speaking of parties, they are the perfect opportunity to display your creativity in gift packaging. Take a large, plain basket, such as this laundry basket and wrap a colorful cloth around it, tying the ends together at each corner in a substantial knot. Tuck the loose ends under or within the knot. This basket is a perfect way to present an armload of gifts to an excited child. The material you use can reflect the theme of the party—a camouflage cloth for a young boy, or lace, chintz, or pretty pastel for a young girl. To delight the whole family, place large fabric-covered baskets under your Christmas tree, and put a number of gifts in each.

A wrapped basket can also easily be used as gift wrap for a holiday plant. Don't forget to line the basket with plastic to prevent damage. A lovely plaid, paisley, or even a metallic fabric might add just the needed touch to a room during a long winter, or dress up the environment during a party. You can substitute paper for fabric, but be careful when securing the corners: paper has a tendency to tear and curl.

Animal Baskets

The idea of using baskets as packaging was what inspired these animal baskets. They are simple nested baskets with wooden extensions attached. For these baskets it is essential to use closely woven baskets that are fairly strong. To construct each animal, you need to find a closely woven nest of baskets that feels somewhat substantial. I traced out the side proportions on tracing paper, then drew the head, tail, legs, and handle grip for the lid. Once the proportions seemed right and I felt the legs and feet would hold the animal, I cut the pieces from one-quarter-inch lumber. Plywood would certainly do. To attach the wood to the basket, place a thin piece of wood against the inside of the basket so that the nail goes through the wood, then into the basket and into the cut shape that forms the body part. That added piece of wood on the inside of the basket is essential to the structure of this design. When adding the legs, angle the hind legs out, so that the basket doesn't tip over. The slight flair acts as a stronger support. Paint the baskets with bright, highly-patterned designs using acrylic paint and give them to a young child for his or her birthday. They will remember your effort, and you will remember their pleasurable surprise.

Personalized Duck Baskets

Often you can examine a basket, and with very little effort change it to become a more personal gift. The three colorful ducks are baskets that have simply been repainted with new button eyes added, and yet their character changes as they become personalized. What a good gift they would make for a new baby, with lots of baby supplies tucked within. Painting the basket with acrylic paint takes two coats. Using a one-inch oil paint brush you can simply paint them opaque as I have done. Or try out some of the printing techniques that have been described within this book, such as antiquing them with a gentle wash of color, or stenciling a child's name on the side of the duck's body, or freehand painting a garden of magical flowers.

Young children will find these ducks handy companions and they can be useful aids for teaching them how to keep small toys in neat order. The duck is only one of many animal and bird shapes that are made in China, and woven with a sculptural contour. A menagerie of baskets would make any child's room extra special.

Use a color wheel as a reference and paint each bird a primary color, or all the animals different shades of one color. Stencil numbers or ABC's on them and stand them in a row. Replace the tiny glass eyes that come with the basket (they come unglued very easily) with big buttons. Buy the buttons at a fabric store or a five-and-dime. Allow your imagination to roam, and you'll discover charming answers to your creative questions. The duck baskets could also be gilded and filled with flowers.

Easter Basket

The traditional Easter basket could easily become something very special. Throughout his younger years, our son found his Easter basket filled with a straw bed on which his eggs and chocolate surprises were laid.

The basket itself was an antique, and we kept it throughout the year as part of our home decor. As he moves from home and begins his own family, I would hope this basket would move with him, thus continuing the same tradition. Giving an Easter basket is another instance when one can be creative by adding something new to a regular tradition.

One year my wife received an Easter basket filled with fresh flowers and foil-covered eggs, much like the one illustrated here. To keep flowers fresh, you must buy a few water tubes, or water picks from your local florist; they all have them. Plan to decorate a basket that is woven in such a way that you can insert the ends of the water tubes into the woven structure of the basket without destroying it. Small florist wire will help keep the tubes upright. At the same time you have to hide the tubes. You can always use a few pieces of moss to cover the tubes. Secure the moss to the basket with a hot glue gun. I find that when making something that involves fresh flowers, it is best to cluster the flowers in small constellations around the basket rim, or on the handle. This clustering unites the focus and adds to the overall sweetness and festive feeling. If the water evaporates, the flowers can be removed and placed in a tea cup which has a greater capacity for water, or allowed to dry in the tubes. Many flowers will hold some of their natural color and the now empty basket will remain a reminder of a very special day and your thoughtfulness to someone special to you.

Clay Pot Basket

Within these pages I have tried to give you ideas that would be easy to duplicate, understand, and master. One of the most widely available baskets that exists for holding a clay pot is the one illustrated at right. This basket comes in a number of sizes and is generally a medium dark natural color. To spruce up your holiday environment, you can spray paint the basket gold or silver, or paint it another color that works well with your room. Add a satin bow. The ivy wreath is equally easy to duplicate. I took a hanging ivy plant purchased at my local florist, undid the coat hanger and rebent the wire into a ring and twisted the remaining portion together. You may want to cut off some of the length, which you can do with regular wire cutters. Insert the twisted end into the pot-ted ivy, trying not to mash the root system. I favor the edge of the pot. Take the longest ivy vines and gently pull them up toward the top of the ring. Tie them to the ring with small lengths of covered wire garbage bag "twisties," making sure you leave sufficient room for the plant to move and grow. Continue this process until the wreath reaches proper fullness. Then add a candle, but be very careful that it doesn't burn the plant and start a fire.

There are so many ways of decorating a basket. Take the old ones from your attic or garage and reuse them. Give them a new coat of color or remake them with any combination of the techniques discussed in this book. Test your creativity by enjoying the basic pleasures of making or decorating a basket.

Special Occasion Baskets

Baskets are remarkable, timeless forms. They can be simply placed on a table or arranged along a mantle-piece for the pure pleasure derived from their individual beauty. However, baskets are functional forms as well. They can be used for picnics, holding knick-knacks, or displaying breads or fruits at a dinner party. In fact, the list is virtually endless. This chapter takes a look at the many creative ways you can use and display your favorite old baskets, your handmade ones, or those you have customized.

This composition of Shaker-styled baskets is marked by an overall unity and subtlety. Their shapes and textures soothe the eye and fill the horizontal line of the mantlepiece, not only with volume, but with a quieting power and calming presence. These four baskets are actually reproductions made in China, yet they still carry quaint presence of ancient Shaker tradition. In a composition such as this, I will often add a contrasting Asian, African, or a Southwest Native American basket to juxtapose styles and forms.

In today's culture many people use baskets primarily for pure decoration. They hang antique baskets from kitchen beams or place them on top of country pie safes. They place them on mantlepieces or arrange them on antique tables. This abundant use of antique baskets as display items has elevated the basket craftsman's art to pure aesthetic appreciation.

What is important in all of this is that we are using baskets as companions to daily living. They grace our lives and bring to us a sense of the past, within our modern, diverse, and distant world. Baskets are historical items. So within our lives, baskets can be used throughout our homes fulfilling any number of functions. When house guests arrive, lay out their towels and fresh soap in a wire basket that can easily be taken into the shower. Thus, you offer a bit of hospitality in a charming way. For the bathroom, this modern vinyl coated wire basket seems the perfect solution to holding soaps and shampoos. The basket can be used time and again as the wire structure is impervious to moisture.

I like to use baskets that have come from my travels, combining baskets that are of similar shapes, but not necessarily of the same origin. The baskets (page 102, 103) that hold bathroom towels and dried roses were brought from the subcontinent of India. Tea pickers of Assam used the larger basket filled with towels, while the people from the Sind desert of Pakistan carried the two smaller baskets. I find they make perfect storage vessels.

Dining is a time when the traditional bread basket usually appears on the table. With more casual dining and the upsurge of personal style, the basket has taken on a greater prominence in food presentation and tabletop decor. Casual dinners in front

of raging fires, quiet luncheons, or the sought-after breakfast in bed, are all good times to use baskets. You can wrap up foods to keep them warm or just display foods to great advantage within a beautiful basket. A picnic is a traditional time to pack up a basket and head for the elements. Handled baskets make carrying salads and plates and utensils so much easier than when everything is separate. Set your table using low, woven plate liners and a garden basket filled with small plants as a centerpiece. Change the plants to cactus for a Southwest feeling, or African violets during winter months, and use small baskets to hold condiments.

Baskets are equally useful for parties and special occasions. They can be used as hampers or trays for linens and breads. Serving bowls can be placed inside handled baskets to bring a new twist to the art of passing food.

The kitchen is a handy place to retain a few chosen working baskets. There is a difference between those baskets that are used for special occasions and those that are used daily. Keeping kitchen spoons in a basket either hung by the stove or placed on the counter, provides you with a handy location for often-used utensils. Don't be timid about using baskets; they are natural containers. Baskets will warm and enrich most environments. I have always loved baskets hanging from country kitchen beams, but I get even more pleasure if I see that they are being used everyday.

If you are planning a party with a theme or preparing for a holiday gathering of family and friends, use a basket as holder for votive candles. Line a low, flat basket with heavy-duty aluminum foil and then fill it with about one inch of sand. Carefully place the candles into the sand and add clear marbles or small pebbles to keep them in place. As with any candle, always remember to extinguish the flames before leaving the room where the candles are burning. This tray of votive candles work well as a centerpiece on a coffee table or a sideboard. Another option is to use a larger basket and fill it with fruits. Carve out the top piece of fruit (see the pumpkin on page 115) to hold a votive candle. The basket makes a great focal point for your table or buffet.

Often the big question is, is this the right situation to use a basket? There might be times when you hesitate, but if your instincts say yes, it is best to try. You may be pleasantly surprised with the outcome.

While shopping at the local nursery, I discovered delicate bulb flowers that did not require any water or soil to grow. They seemed very much at home when placed in a long, thin woven tray with rocks nested around them. This still life is a unique, charming, miniature landscape that is maintenance free.

Placing a basket outside is a tricky prospect. Rain and sunlight will eventually dry out the basket fibers, making it brittle and more susceptible to damage. You can, however, seal a woven basket with a poly protection and put it in a place where the elements don't hit it directly. Some baskets are so inexpensive that you can use them for one season, deriving enormous pleasure from them, and then not worry so much if they need replacing down the road. Obviously, if a basket has a great amount of sentimental value, it would be unwise to subject it to any harmful situations that would destroy it.

Many different types of wire baskets (such as this milkman's basket) can also be filled and used in a number of ways. If you are having a party, pick a few stems of flowers from your garden and place the individual stems into separate milk bottles in the carrying basket. This decoration makes a wonderful table setting. Other variations on this theme can be achieved by using Mason jars, antique apothecary jars, or colored glass bottles instead of the old milk bottles.

As mentioned earlier, planting a basket with summer or fall flowers makes a lovely arrangement. Remember, however, to line the basket with plastic to protect it from the soil and water. Then change plants as the season changes. The main point to planting a basket is to protect the basket from excessive moisture. Do then plant directly into the basket, but use it as the outer shell to cover the actual planting construction.

Hanging baskets work well for a front door or the side of a porch or fence. Ask the advice of your local nursery and choose flowers that will work best for your area and particular placement. Take into consideration where you intend to hang the basket and ask what quality of sunlight it should receive. The porch is a natural place for keeping baskets with plants, large or small. Both painted and natural baskets work well with the atmosphere of a cozy porch.

Throughout the winter, birds that remain in my area love to dine off the giant sunflowers that I save from my garden. Each year I place a group of them in a basket near my back steps and replace the sunflowers as the seeds are eaten. As the winter intensifies, I usually change the menu for the birds introducing halves of oranges, suet, and other seeds. This traditional split-wood basket with a decorative handle makes a simple bird feeder that is as visually pleasing as it is useful.

I have written earlier about the use of candles in baskets. This basket made from a pumpkin, provides a very unusual candle holder. The candles are placed into the hollow of the baby pumpkin and lit for the duration of the party. (Always beware of their burning power.) The pumpkin basket is a simple yet delightful solution for holding flowers. To make this container, first cut the top of a flat, sitting pumpkin and clean out the inside. Cut a hole into each side of the pumpkin about three inches down from the top opening. Slide one end of the grapevine into the hole on one side of the pumpkin and bend it up and over, inserting the other end into the second hole. You should now have a pumpkin with a handle. Take the additional grapevine, with some of the leaves remaining, and wrap them around the top of the pumpkin. This adds a collar to the pumpkin and anchors the handle in place. To hold the flowers, sim-

ply wash out a coffee can or a large glass or plastic jar and insert it into the pumpkin. Arrange the garden flowers and call your guests. A number of fruits and vegetables also make charming containers for flowers. Try using squash, eggplant, or a variety of melons. Cut a small hole in the fruit or vegetable and arrange the fresh flowers. Carving a handle on a watermelon is relatively easy and quick to do, but you should practice before committing your knife to a melon that has a party destination. Breads, too, offer many possibilities for becoming a great basket centerpiece. Perhaps a good reminder when experimenting with non-traditional basket forms is that if you are going to place anything within them that is moist, add a foil or plastic liner first. And, if you are doing this for a special function, try it out well before the party time so you have time to solve any problems that might occur.

Baskets are the traditional vessel for offering flowers on Mother's Day, as well as for giving a gift of fruit. How a gift looks is almost as important as what the actual gift is. This fruit basket brings its own well wishes with the rich blending of colors and the juxtaposition of fruits. Add a box of raspberries to give the surprise that extra touch. Most major food markets have a great selection of fresh fruits, but why settle only on fruit. Fill your basket with vegetables or a combination of fruits and vegetables as the perfect winter gift. Another lovely addition would be a freesia or a rose. By using water picks, available at any nursery or craft store, the flowers will stay fresh and beautiful for much, much longer. Simply fill the water pick with water, insert the stem of the flower, and bury the pick among the basket contents. The flower will add a refreshing departure from the three-grapefruit cluster of bananas and a pineapple that has dominated pre-made gift baskets for years.

A variation to the fruit, vegetable, and flowers theme is to create a gift basket cheeses and breads. Combine a variety of cheeses, some flowers, and an array of freshly made breads or crackers into a long basket with two handles. Varying the shape and size of your basket choice may inspire you to alter the ingredients. Who would not enjoy someone appearing at their door with a basket filled with many flavors of ice cream? Another possibility is to include a delicious tart or a great heap of pastries. Guests at a party will enjoy being served from the basket and the host will remember your thoughtfulness when reusing the basket.

This split-wood garden basket is another example of using a basket as a gift wrap. The basket itself has been painted many shades of red, from a light pink to the deepest plum red. Rose hips have been added to extend the overall color scheme. The gift is wrapped in a pale pink paper and tied with a deeper pink bow. Another option is to use the basket as the actual gift box. To do this, lay a length of ribbon inside the basket, then place a few sheets of tissue paper on the ribbon. Next, place the gift on the tissue and fold the tissue around the gift and securely tie a bow with the ribbon.

Think of a basket as a replacement for a box, and invent your own combination of wrapping designs. Give the members of your family a gift within a basket for Christmas, and carry that theme throughout much of your home decoration. Place small wire baskets filled with sweets, candies, or small freshly baked cookies under your tree for party guests to take home with them. Great baskets of fresh boughs will bring the rich aroma of the forest through many rooms of your home and use more little wire baskets as place markers at the dinner table. There is a wide variety of delicate small baskets available in craft stores and florist shops. Frequent these places and see what is new, for it is so easy to find ample party and holiday ideas there.

Another way to use miniature baskets during the holidays, is to hang them from a freshly made boxwood topiary. The topiary is very easy to construct. You will need a styrofoam ball about the size of a hard ball, three to four inches in width, another piece of styrofoam to wedge into a clay pot for its base, and a small branch or even a wooden dowel, for a trunk.

First wedge the styrofoam into the clay pot. Insert the stick or dowel. If you feel the need to secure the stick more tightly, you can do so with a little glue from your hot glue gun. Then press the styrofoam ball down upon the stick so that it is solid and secure. Break off small pieces of boxwood about one and a half inches long and insert them into the ball. Fill the entire ball with the boxwood. Tie pieces of wire to each of the small baskets and insert the wire in the styrofoam ball. When all the baskets are in place, add some boxwood or moss to the base and fill the baskets with holiday candy.

While the largest baskets are appropriate for laundry and for keeping wood by the fireplace, the smallest seem just right for a special gift. Each size, every style, the old and the new, all share a similar thread with the great practice of basket making. Modern craftsmen still retain the ancient rhythms of basket making and the knowledge that their work is rooted in tradition.

The world of how to use baskets, how to fill, and how to decorate baskets is wide and open. Try your hand at making a basket from scratch; begin with a kit, or forge boldly with a twig or vine creation. Or take an old basket and apply some paint, making it your handiwork. Fill one for a gift or add the same to your home for the pleasure of its shape and form. Become a part of the great tradition born of the basket maker.

SOURCES

Aleene's Thick Designer Tacky Glue
Aleene's Artist Inc.
Box 407
Solvang, CA 93463

Basketville, Inc.
Main Street
PO Box 710
Putney, VT 05346

Commonwealth Manufacturing Co.
5-05 48th Avenue
Long Island City, NY 11101

Hallmark Cards,Inc.
25th and McGee
Kansas City, MO 64141

John Milton
Creative Twist
MPR Associates, Inc.
PO Box 7343
High Point, NC 27264

Nadler Enterprises, Inc.
PO Box 1747
Stone Mountain, GA 30086

H.H. Perkins Co.
10 South Bradley Road
Woodbridge, CT 06525

Texas Baskets, Co.
PO Box 1110
Jacksonville, TX 75766

Thermogrip hot melt glue gun
Thermogrip glue sticks
c/o Emhart Home Products Division
PO Box 13716
Reading, PA 19612

Thumbprint Antiques
Old Tongore Road
Stone Ridge, NY 10142

Wildwoods Basketry
3554 Paul Sweet Road
Santa Cruz, CA 95065

INDEX

Aesthetic integrity, 10
Animal baskets, 89–90
Antiquing, 44–46
Apothecary jars, 110
Art, baskets as works of, 10

Bark cone baskets, 34
Basketry, history of, 11
Basketry kits, 22
Bathroom, baskets for, 101
Birdfeeders, 112
Bottles, 110
Bough basket, 121
Boxwood topiaries, 122
Bread basket, 101–4, 114
Bulb flowers, 109
Bushel basket, 73

Candle holders, baskets as, 106, 114
Cheese and bread basket, 117
Christmas basket, 121
Claw hammers, 18
Clay pot basket, 94
Coil baskets, 22–25
Colored glass bottles, 110
Colors, in sewn-pattern baskets, 77
Cone baskets, 34
Cookie basket, 121
Craftsmen, 11
Cut-out basket, 78

Decoration, baskets for, 99
Dinner table, bread basket for, 101–4
Doily basket, 58
Duck basket, 90

Easter basket, 8, 93
Eggplant basket, 114

Fabric Gift basket, 86
Fabric-lined Picnic basket, 52–55
Flower basket, 112
Flowers, 67, 109, 112, 114, 117
Food, baskets for, 101–4, 121
Fruit basket, 117

Gardening clippers, 18
Gift baskets, 49–50, 86, 117, 118
Gift wrapping, baskets as, 118
Gifts, baskets to hold, 118, 121

Hanging baskets, 112
Harvest basket, 62
Heart basket, 80
Hot glue gun, 19

Ice cream basket, 117
Interior design, baskets in, 10

Jars, 110

Kitchen, baskets for, 104
Knives, 18

Large baskets, 125
Laundry baskets, 9, 125
Light, in work areas, 16
Living baskets, 37–38, 42
Log cabin baskets, 30–33

Mason jars, 110
Materials, 16–19
Melon basket, 83, 114
Milkman's basket, 110
Miniature baskets, 122
Moss-covered Mushroom basket, 61
Mother's Day basket, 117
Mushroom basket, 61

Native American basket, 9, 99
Needle nose pliers, 18
Nest basket, 85

Outdoor basket placement, 110

Paint, 46, 68, 73, 74, 85, 89, 90
Paintbrushes, 18
Painted baskets, 55, 58
Parties, baskets for, 104, 106
Pastry basket, 117
Patterned Quilt basket, 74
Personalized Duck basket, 90
Picnic basket, 52–55, 104
Pie basket, 68–71
Plan development, 21
Planting baskets, 37–38, 42
Plastics, 10
Pom Pom Nest basket, 85
Porches, baskets for, 112
Pot basket, 94
Pumpkin basket, 114

Quilt basket, 74

Raffia, 25
Ribbon basket, 55

Sandpaper, 18
Scissors, 18
Screwdrivers, 18
Seashell basket, 64–67
Sewn-pattern basket, 77
Shaker baskets, 99
Split-wood basket, 112, 118
Split-wood Heart basket, 80
Sponged Bushel basket, 73
Spray-paint Doily basket, 58
Spray-paint Ribbon basket, 55
Squash basket, 114
Stain, 46
Stenciled Pie basket, 68–71
Stencils, 74

Stone-finish Tray basket, 55
Storage space, 19
Styrofoam, 122

Tools, 16–19
Topiaries, 122
Towels, baskets for holding, 101
Tray basket, 55
Twig baskets, 33

Utility, of baskets, 10, 12

Vegetable basket, 117
Vegetables, baskets made from, 114
Vine baskets, 27–28
Vinyl-covered Wire basket, 101
Votive candles, baskets as holders for, 106

Watermelon basket, 83, 114
Wire basket, 101, 110, 121
Wire cutters, 18
Wire planting baskets, 37–38
Wooden Cut-out basket, 78
Work areas, 16
Wrapped basket, 86

Special thanks to the following people:

To Elli Schneider of Offray Ribbons for the beautiful ribbons that adorn the baskets.
Offray ribbon offers the most complete range of quality ribbons.

To Martin Swanson President of Texas Baskets for generously providing me with a number of baskets made by Texas Basket Company. Your cooperation is always greatly appreciated.

To Shirley Ellis of Basketville who provided baskets that were essential to the make up of the book. Basketville stores have such a tremendous selection of baskets from the world to choose from.

To Mark DeFrancesso of H.H. Perkins Company for the basket kit and samples of materials that make up the diverse range of products by H.H. Perkins Company.

To John Milton, President of MPR Associates, Inc., makers of Creative Twist the versatile paper product that makes any basket or anything else something special.

To Robert Palmatier and Fredric Misner for the many antiques from their Stone Ridge antique shop, and for the grapevine that found its way into baskets.

To Michael DeMent of Hallmark Cards, Inc for paper and candle accessories used throughout the book.

To John Riccardi and Rudy Grant of Seagroatt Floral Supply Company for their dried and fresh roses. They were a beautiful addition to the book.

To Donald Gonclaves of Emheart Home Products Division for providing me with a Thermogrip brand hot melt Glue gun. I find the product absolutely essential for working with baskets.

To Aleene for providing her thick designer tacky glue. Many projects simply rely on the use of this product.

To Nancy Jones of Bob's Candy for providing the candy canes and holiday candies used in the book.